Have Fun with Farting Ron

Thank you for purchasing this book.

I would be very grateful if you would like to leave an honest review of this book.

Copyright 2021 by Smile Melody. All rights reserved. No part of this book may be reproduced in any form without permission in writing from the publisher.

This book belongs to:

....

Hi. My name is Ron, and I am a raptor. I am a happy dinosaur who likes jokes.

Let me tell you my secret. When something makes me laugh a lot, I make big farts.

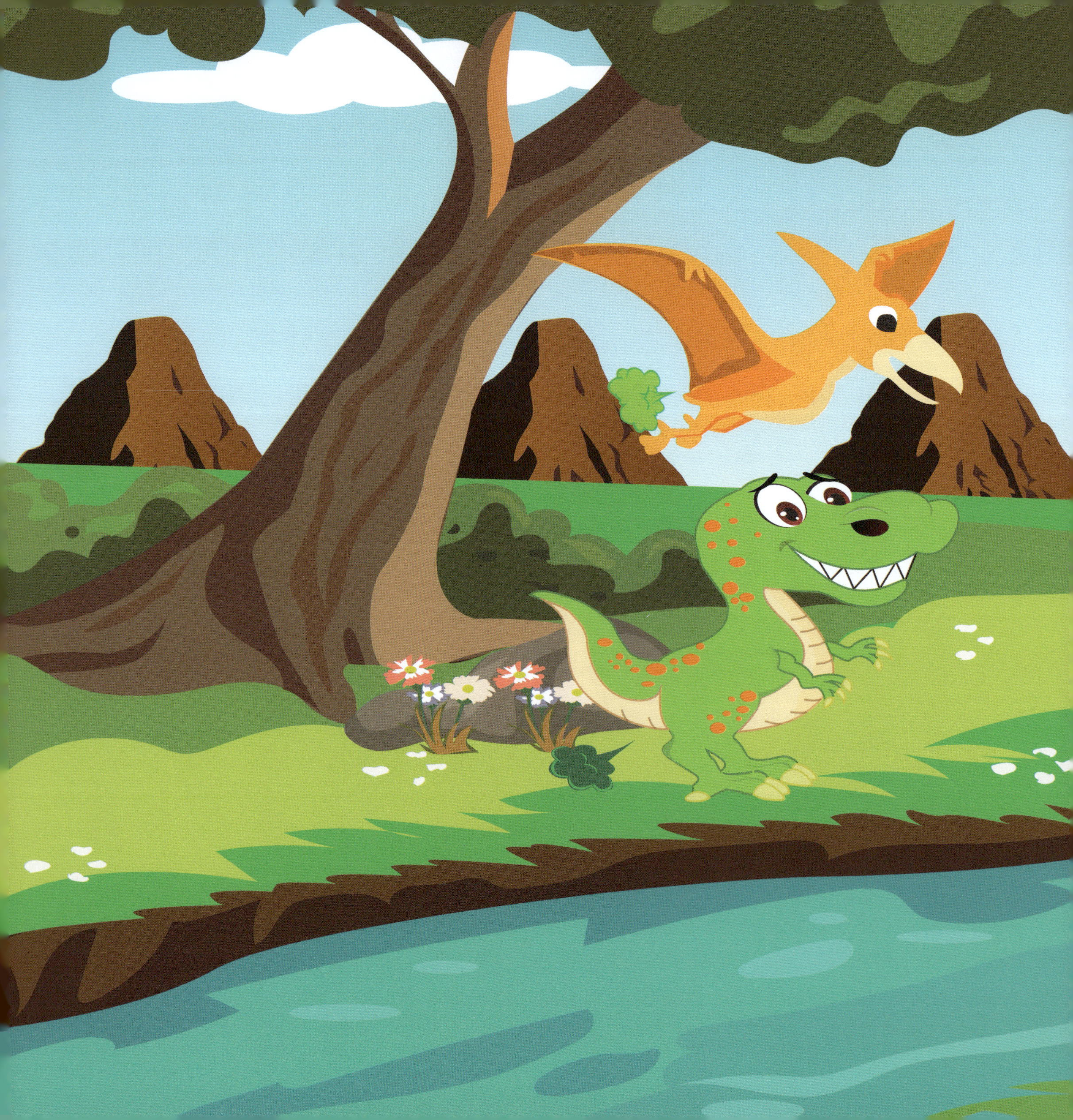

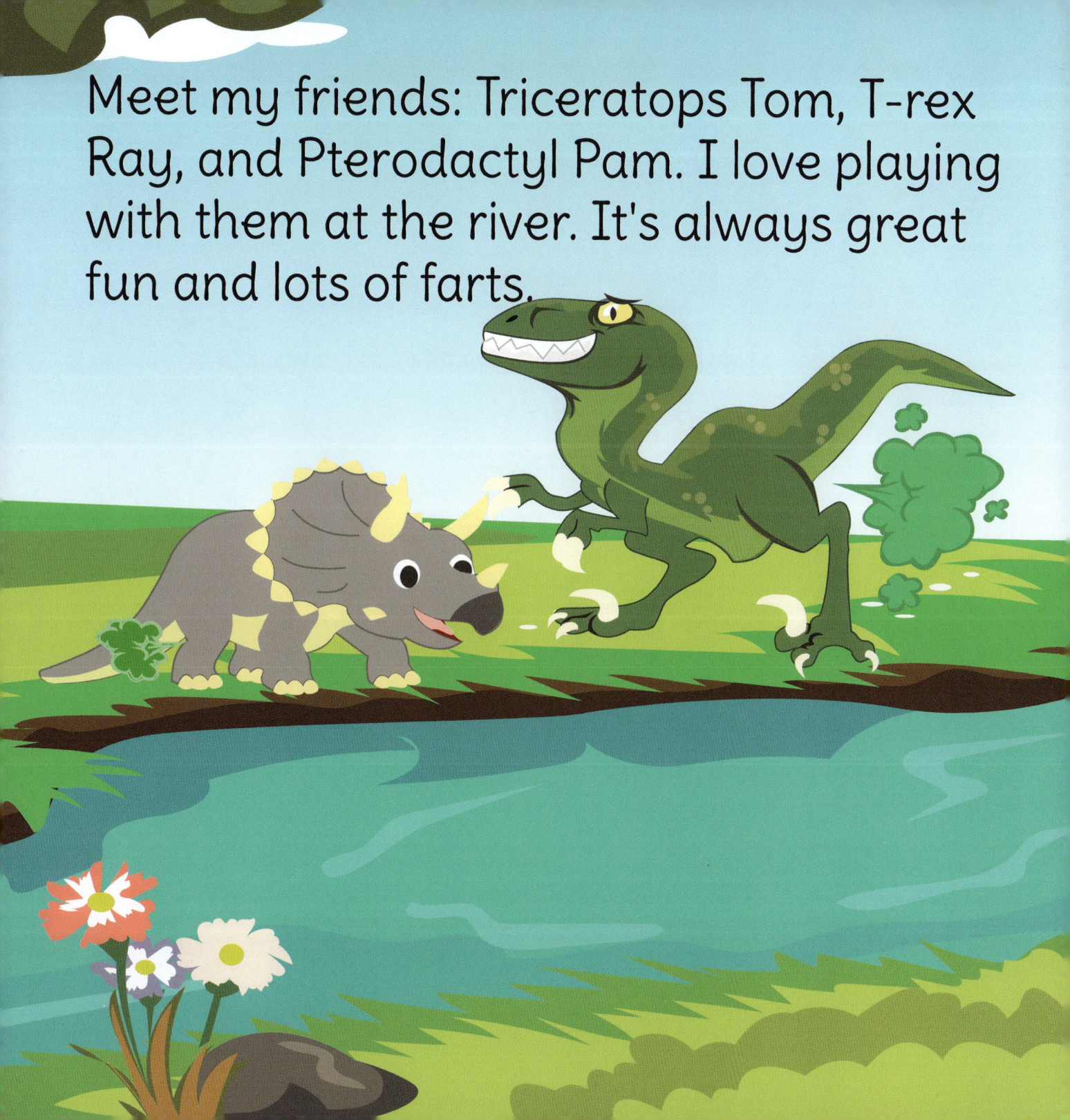

Meet my friends: Triceratops Tom, T-rex Ray, and Pterodactyl Pam. I love playing with them at the river. It's always great fun and lots of farts.

I have a dream to take part in the World Farting Championship.

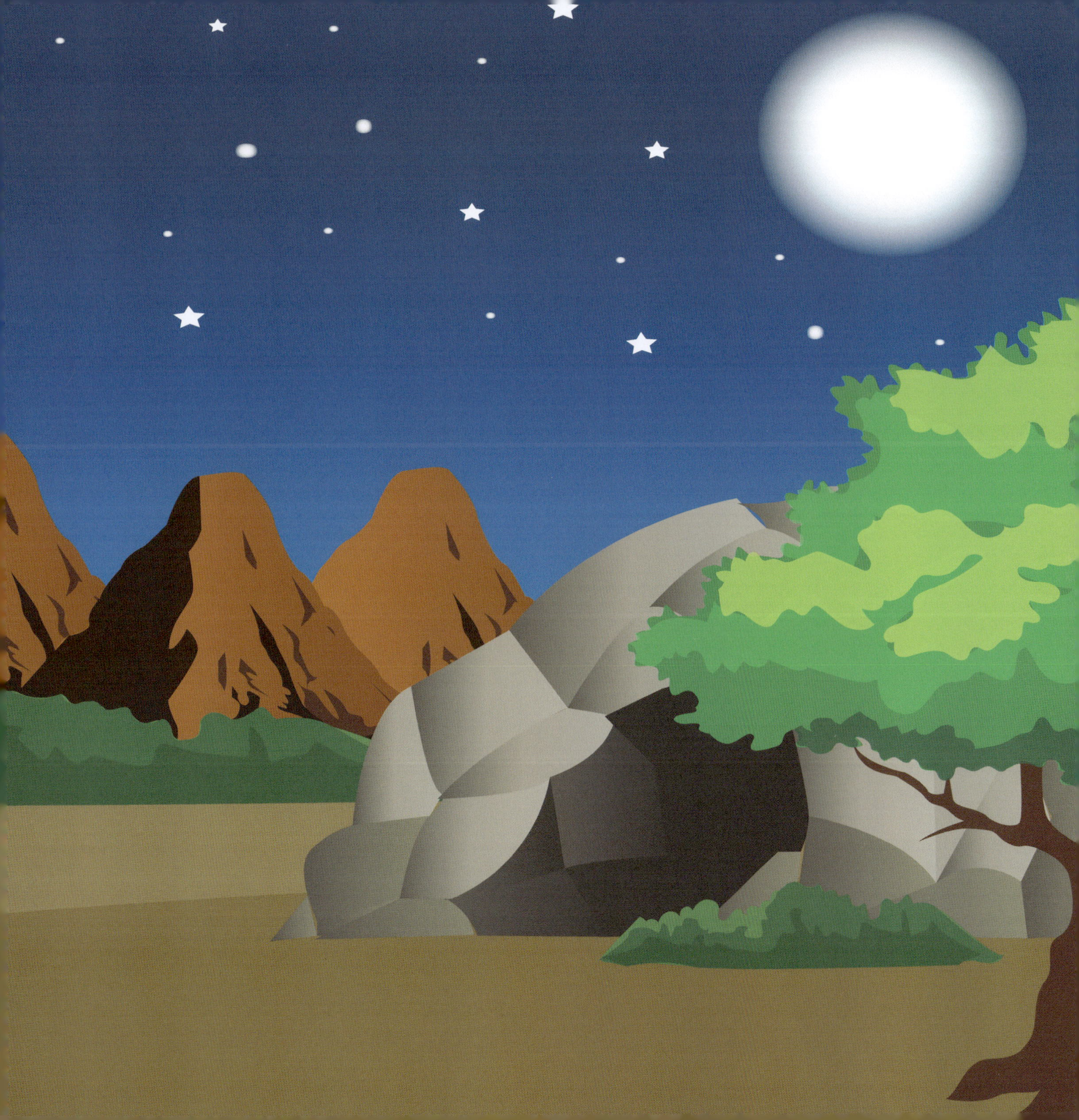

My dad likes to tell jokes. What is the name of the dinosaur who likes chickens? - he asked.

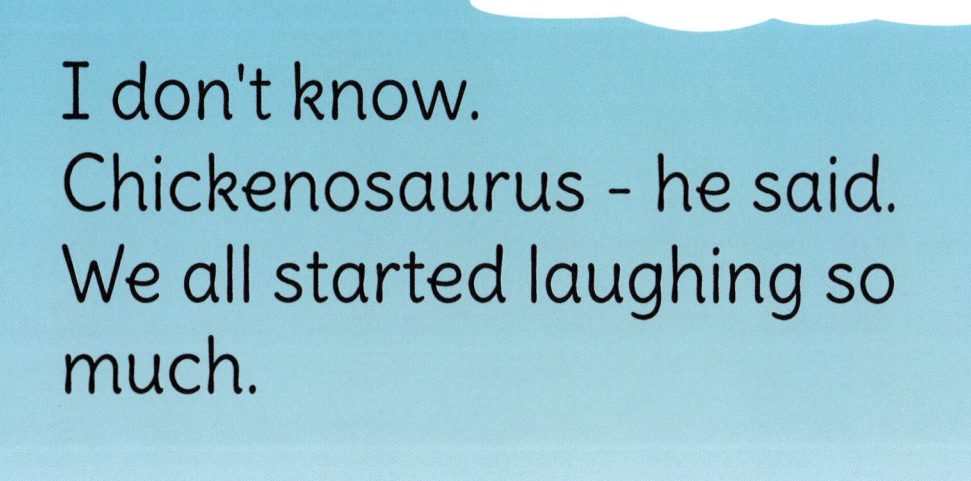

I don't know. Chickenosaurus - he said. We all started laughing so much.

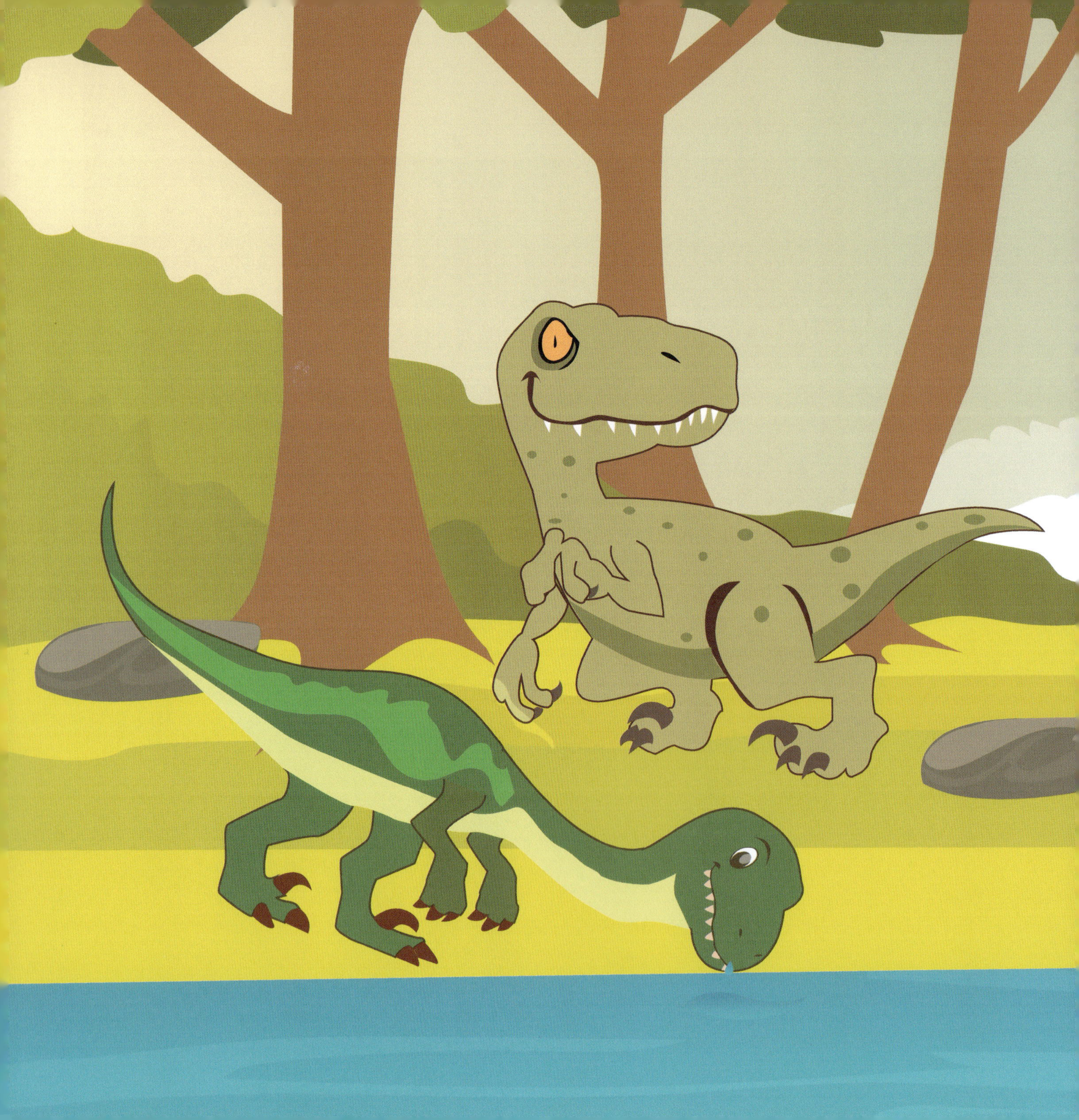

I think I have a talent for farting,
so I would like to participate in the
upcoming World Farting Championship.
You have our support - my parents said.
I was happy to hear these words.

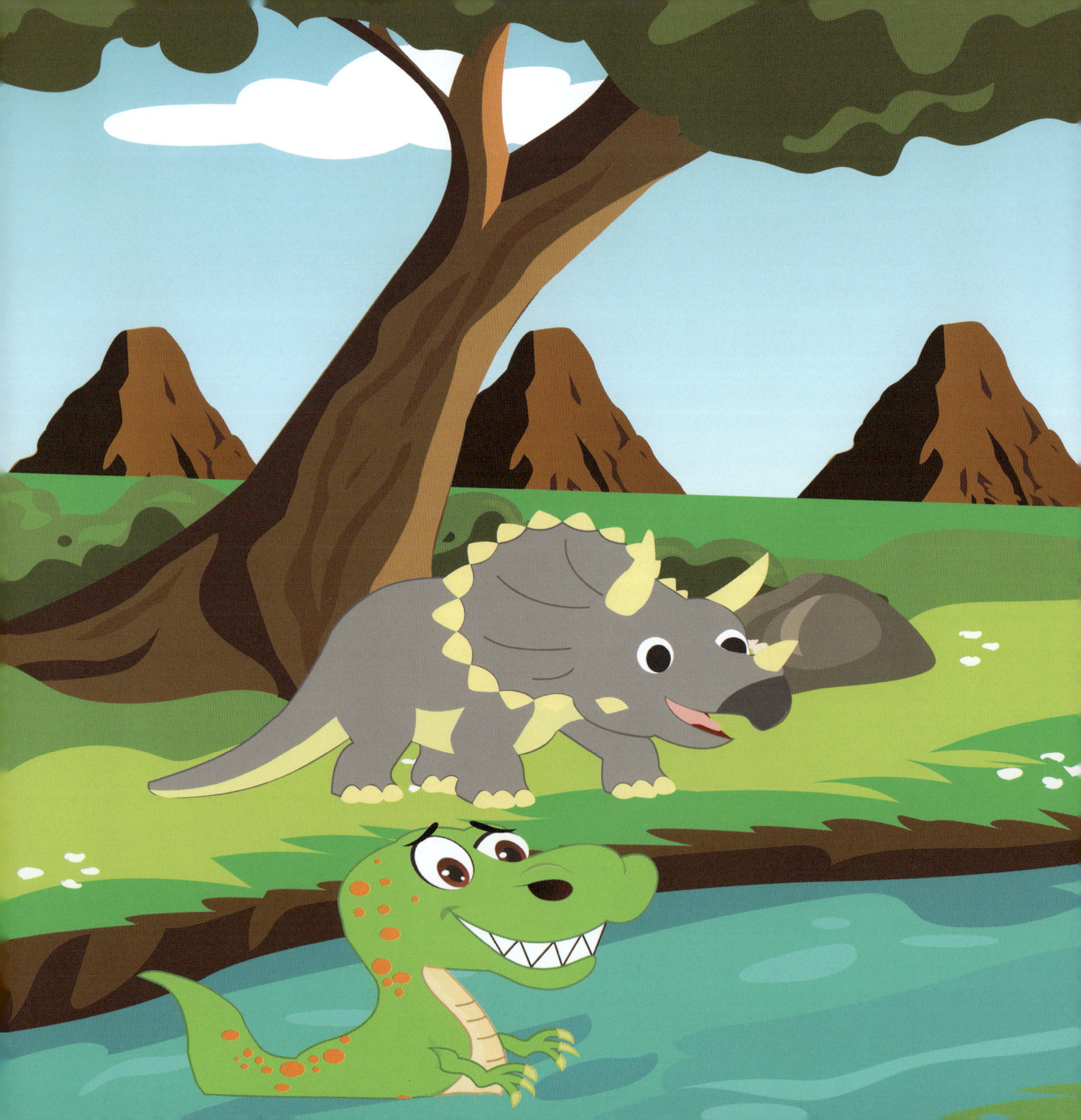

What a big bubble fart RON!!!

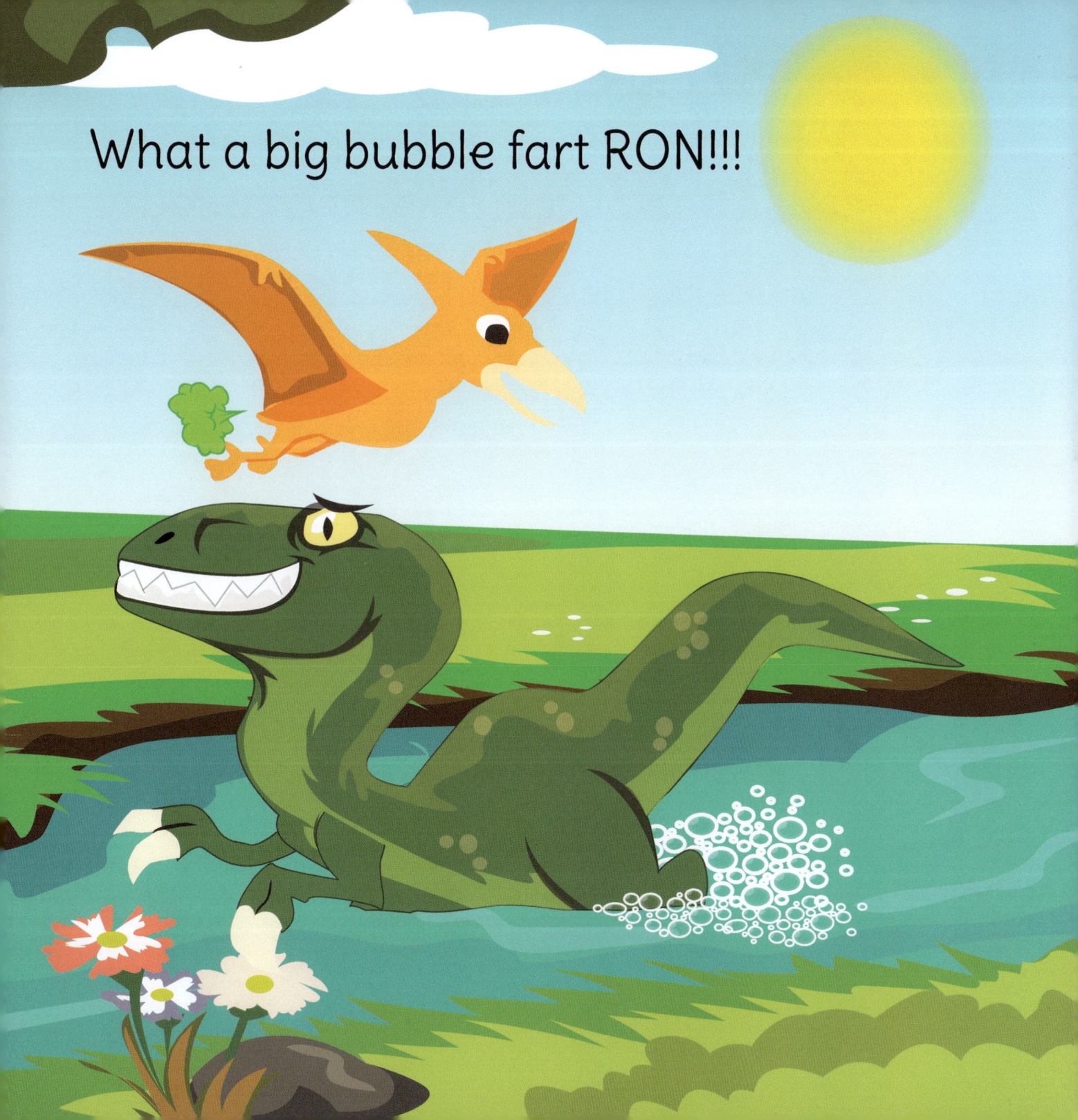

The long-awaited day has come. The Championship Arena has impressed me. Please keep your fingers crossed for me.

The Farting Championship

The judges for today's Championship will be the multiple World Champion T-Rex, the experienced Ankylosaurus, and the equally successful Triceratops.

They will award a score from 1 to 10 points for each performance. Whoever earns more points wins and moves on to the next round.

My first opponent was Spinosaurus. I was stressed before my first fight. My friends helped me and made me laugh so much that I let out a big green fart.

I received the score: 7, 8, 7. I defeated my opponent and moved on to the next round.

My second opponent is the Diplodocus. The dinosaur with a long neck and tail. Even though he was much bigger than me, I was not afraid.

I was confident that I could win against him. I got a better score and advanced to the quarterfinals.

The stress was getting worse. My quarterfinal opponent was a Stegosaurus. Facing me was a strong dinosaur with spikes on its tail and distinctive plates on its back.

I focused on my goal and let out a big fart.
I won and advanced to the semifinals.

In the semifinals, my opponent was the flying dinosaur Pterodactyl. I realized that only one win separated me from the grand final.

I had the support of my friends in this unique moment. They told me a funny joke. I laughed so hard that I received 10, 9, 9 points for my fart and advanced to the final.

Mom! Dad! I advanced to the grand finals of the World Farting Championship!

Grand Final

My final battle was against the son of the Grand Champion.
T-rex started the fight and scored 10, 9, 9 for his fart. It was a good score.

I closed my eyes and thought it was the most important moment in my life. When I opened my eyes, I let out the biggest fart ever.
I received 10, 10, 10 points and became the New World Champion.

YEAH!!! I am the WORLD CHAMPION!!!

DREAMS COME TRUE

1

Printed in Great Britain
by Amazon